HALLOWEEN

P9-CFD-829

POEMS OF HALLOWEEN NIGHT
RAGGED SHADOWS

Selected by Lee Bennett Hopkins
Illustrated by
Giles Laroche

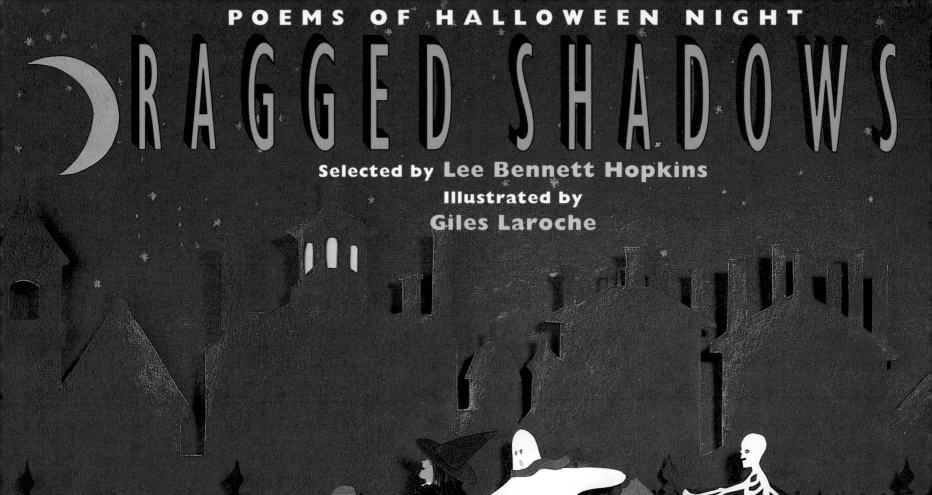

Little, Brown and Company
Boston Toronto London

For Lucy and Kevin Boyd —
Forever-Treats
L. B. H.

For the children of Salem
G. L.

First Edition

Copyright acknowledgments appear on page 32.

Library of Congress Cataloging-in-Publication Data

Ragged shadows : poems of Halloween night / selected by Lee Bennett Hopkins ;
    illustrated by Giles Laroche. — 1st ed.
        p.   cm.
    Summary: A collection of poems about Halloween and its creatures, by such authors as Jane Yolen, Karla Kuskin, and Nancy Willard.
    ISBN 0-316-37276-5
    1. Halloween — Juvenile poetry. 2. Children's poetry, American.
[1. Halloween — Poetry. 2. American poetry — Collections.]
I. Hopkins, Lee Bennett. II. Laroche, Giles, ill.
PS595.H35R34 1993
811.008'033 — dc20   92-1369

10 9 8 7 6 5 4 3 2 1

NIL

Published simultaneously in Canada by Little, Brown & Company (Canada) Limited

Printed in Italy

CONTENTS

HALLOWEEN BEGINS

Night is spun
with spidery singing,
high and thin.
Bare trees bend
their cold bones,
dancing in the wind.

Something
prowls
outside my window.

    Now —
        Again.

Somewhere
in the black-cat dark,
Halloween
begins . . .

TONY JOHNSTON

4

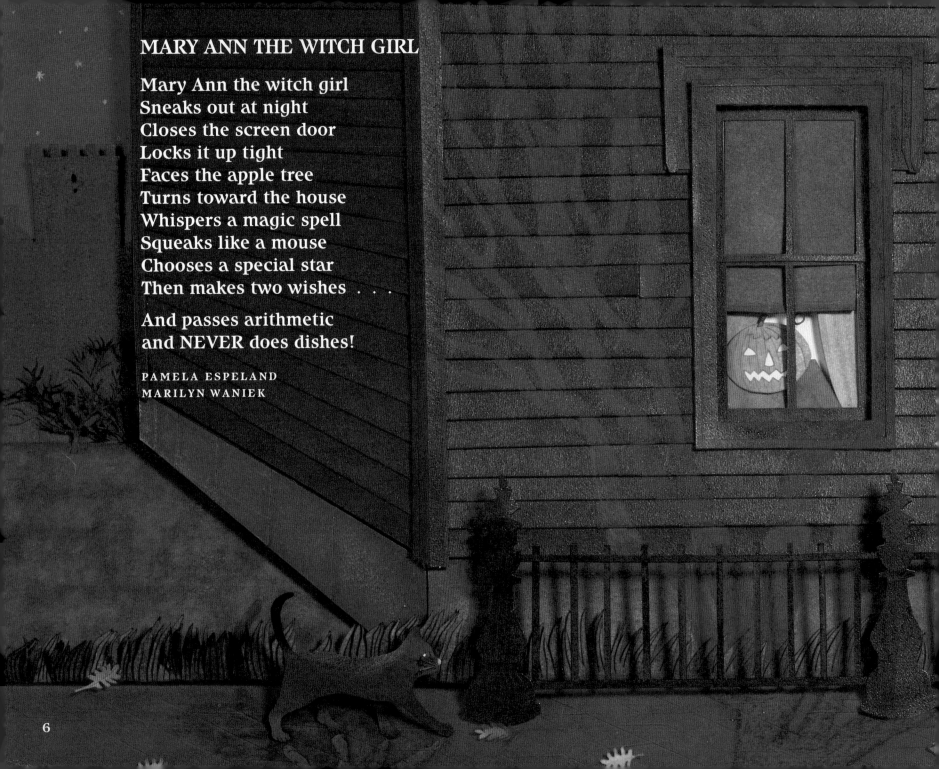

MARY ANN THE WITCH GIRL

Mary Ann the witch girl
Sneaks out at night
Closes the screen door
Locks it up tight
Faces the apple tree
Turns toward the house
Whispers a magic spell
Squeaks like a mouse
Chooses a special star
Then makes two wishes . . .

And passes arithmetic
and NEVER does dishes!

PAMELA ESPELAND
MARILYN WANIEK

SHIVERS

Bushes quiver
where shadows lean,
and not a sliver
of moon is seen.

Near the river
some goblins (green)
with a witch in front
and a ghost between

Make me sh . . i . . vvvver,
but I am keen
about the shivers
of Halloween.

AILEEN FISHER

8

PUMPKIN

After its lid
Is cut, the slick
Seeds and stuck
Wet strings
Scooped out,
Walls scraped
Dry and white,
Face carved, candle
Fixed and lit,

Light creeps
Into the thick
Rind: giving
That dead orange
Vegetable skull
Warm skin, making
A live head
To hold its
Sharp gold grin.

VALERIE WORTH

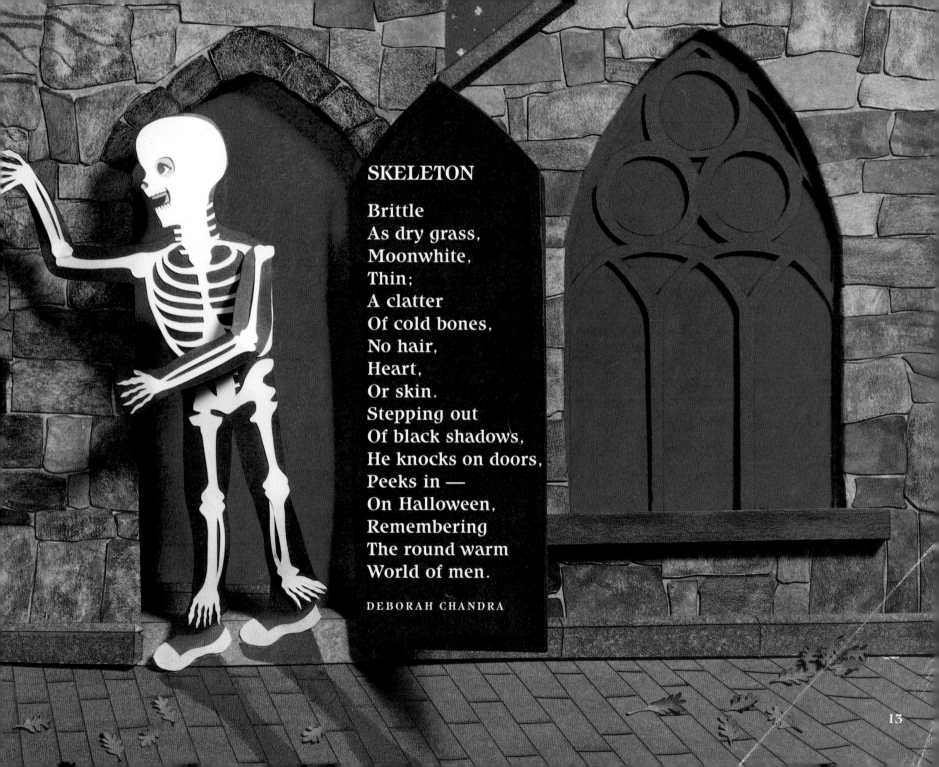

SKELETON

Brittle
As dry grass,
Moonwhite,
Thin;
A clatter
Of cold bones,
No hair,
Heart,
Or skin.
Stepping out
Of black shadows,
He knocks on doors,
Peeks in —
On Halloween,
Remembering
The round warm
World of men.

DEBORAH CHANDRA

13

HALLOWED EVE

Beyond the lawn, beyond the trees,
   night rubs her back against the house,
Moving as a stalking cat
   searching out the frightened mouse
Who scuttles over mounds
   and old gravestones.
Planted in the earth
   their square white bones
Tilt skyward to a spirit moon
   while the wind sing-songs
A devil's tune.

LILLIAN M. FISHER

SKELETON KEY

Does it open a house with a tombstone door
and spiderwebs on the marble floor
under a slab by a graveyard tree —
Is that why they call it a skeleton key?

Do skeletons use them to play their bones
tapping out tunes on xylophones
made of rows of ribs and knobby knees —
Is that why they call them skeleton keys?

Does a skeleton key open *any* door
like mine, at night, when it's hours before
anyone wakes, when no one sees
do they rattle around wherever they please —
Is *that* why they call them skeleton keys?

ALICE SCHERTLE

A HALLOWEEN GHOST STORY

Who lurks there
in the dark?
What hollow tribes
shuffle and whisper
from shadow
to shadow   formless
silent
under the ragged moon?

I will not open my door
to them.
No.
They have counterfeited their tongues
to sound like children
crying TRICK OR TREAT!
TRICK OR . . .
NO! I see the pale mask hiding
cold empty eyes.   I see
the wild hair
blowing.   I see the bone
that presses
the bell!

BARBARA JUSTER ESBENSEN

19

HALLOWEEN GHOST

She's old,
Wind-twisted,
Cobweb soft;
Drifting down
The garden walk,
She stops —
To rearrange her hair,
And straighten threads
Of spirit-cloth.
Silvery threads
That float upon
The dark, like ripples
On a pond
Fading into
Still night air,
Leaving a pool
Of moonlight there.

DEBORAH CHANDRA

20

THE WITCHES' RIDE

Over the hills
Where the edge of the light
Deepens and darkens
To ebony night,
Narrow hats high
Above yellow bead eyes,
The tatter-haired witches
Ride through the skies.
Over the seas
Where the flat fishes sleep
Wrapped in the slap of the slippery deep,
Over the peaks
Where the black trees are bare,
Where boney birds quiver
They glide through the air.
Silently humming
A horrible tune,
They sweep through the stillness
To sit on the moon.

KARLA KUSKIN

HALLOWEEN MOON

A chip of moon,
A broken bone
Is high and silent,
Cold, alone.
But ragged shadows
Dance a tune
The wind sings to
The white bone moon.

FRAN HARAWAY

25

NIGHT SONG

Farewell child
and farewell lamp

cats that wait
at hearth and hole

farewell mole
and farewell bones

thief at gate
and fire on stones

farewell owl
farewell lark —

farewell dark.

NANCY WILLARD

WITCH'S CAT

I am a companion
both dark and light,
I am a shadow
on the edge of sight,
I am a whisper
in the morning grass.
I am a motion
in the tinted glass,
I am a howl
when night is done,
I am a dust mote
in the morning sun,
I am a stroking
beneath your hand,
I am a message
at your command.

JANE YOLEN

12:01 A.M.

No more reason
to
shudder,
shake,

shiver,
tremble,
quiver,
quake.

No more reason
for
throat
to
thirst.

Halloween's
over.

It's
November
FIRST.

LEE BENNETT HOPKINS

31

ACKNOWLEDGMENTS

Thanks are due to the following for works reprinted herein:

Curtis Brown Ltd. for "12:01 A.M.," by Lee Bennett Hopkins, copyright © 1993 by Lee Bennett Hopkins; "Witch's Cat," by Jane Yolen, copyright © 1991 by Jane Yolen. Reprinted by permission of Curtis Brown Ltd. Farrar, Straus & Giroux, Inc. for "Skeleton," from *Balloons and Other Poems*, by Deborah Chandra, copyright © 1988, 1990 by Deborah Chandra; "Pumpkin," from *More Small Poems*, by Valerie Worth, copyright © 1976 by Valerie Worth. Reprinted by permission of Farrar, Straus & Giroux, Inc. HarperCollins Publishers for "A Halloween Ghost Story," from *Cold Stars and Fireflies*, by Barbara Juster Esbensen, copyright © 1984 by Barbara Juster Esbensen; "The Witches' Ride," from *Dogs & Dragons, Trees & Dreams*, by Karla Kuskin, copyright © 1980 by Karla Kuskin. Reprinted by permission of HarperCollins Publishers. Alfred A. Knopf, Inc. for "Night Song," from *Water Walker*, by Nancy Willard, copyright © 1989 by Nancy Willard, reprinted by permission of Alfred A. Knopf, Inc. Deborah Chandra for "Halloween Ghost," Pamela Espeland and Marilyn Waniek for "Mary Ann the Witch Girl," Aileen Fisher for "Shivers," Lillian M. Fisher for "Hallowed Eve," Fran Haraway for "Halloween Moon," Tony Johnston for "Halloween Begins," Alice Schertle for "Skeleton Key," all used by permission of the authors, who control all rights.

JUV
811.008
033   Ragged shadows
Ragged
shadows

DUE DATE
